When Kais Met Toussaint

The slave who led his people to freedom

**Written by Claude Louis, MD
and Kristin K. Louis**

Illustrated by Anastasiia Yezhela

ISBN: 978-1-7378954-3-5 (Hardback)
ISBN: 978-1-7378954-4-2 (Paperback)
ISBN: 978-1-7378954-5-9 (e-book)

To my children Kais, Laelah and Maleah. May you always be proud of your Haitian heritage.

To the children of the world, may you cherish and celebrate those who have fought and given their lives for your freedom.

The school bell rings. "Great work today Tigers!" says Ms. Masse, beaming. "Grab your backpacks, and don't forget to think about your projects for Black History Month! Now, off to the buses."

Excited children fill the halls, rushing to the front doors. Kais, a third grader in Ms. Masse's class, stumbles as a group of older kids rush by him.

"Well, that wasn't too friendly," says a man scooting around a bucket and mop. Kais had seen him before and always thought he had kind eyes. "Oh, and you dropped your book!" On the cover was a picture of Dr. Martin Luther King Jr.

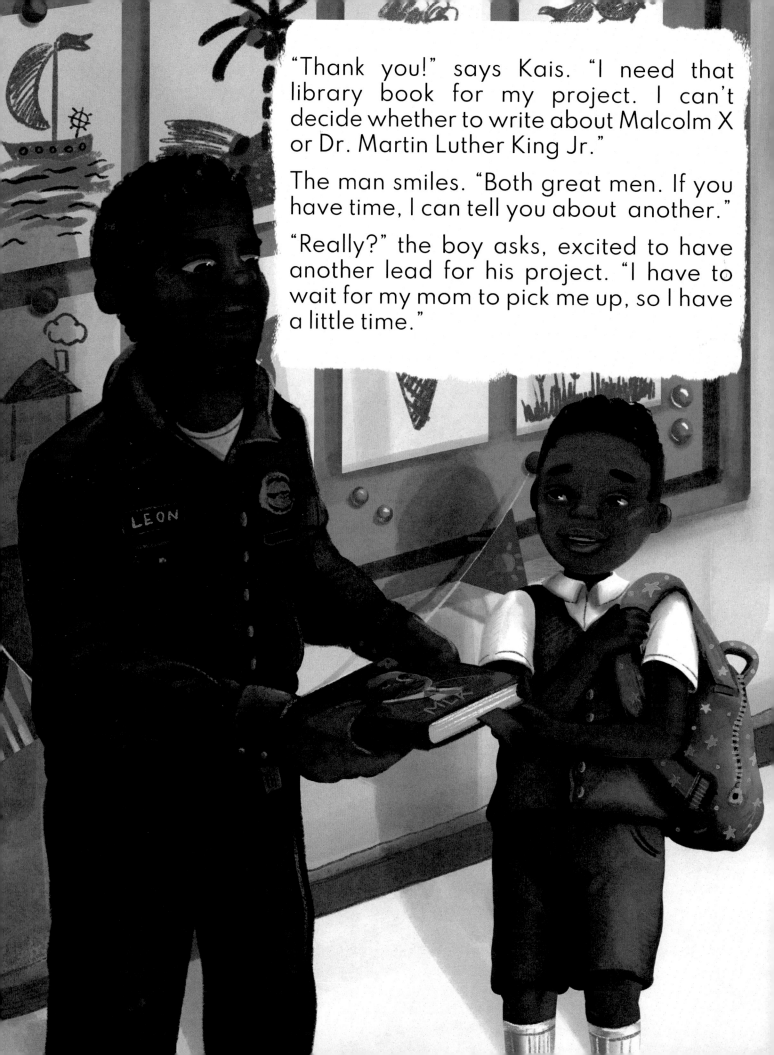

"Thank you!" says Kais. "I need that library book for my project. I can't decide whether to write about Malcolm X or Dr. Martin Luther King Jr."

The man smiles. "Both great men. If you have time, I can tell you about another."

"Really?" the boy asks, excited to have another lead for his project. "I have to wait for my mom to pick me up, so I have a little time."

"Well then," says the man. "You can call me Mr. Leon." He points to the name stitched on his uniform.

"Kais Knight. Nice to meet you."

Mr. Leon nods. "Now, the two people you're considering are great choices. They were both very influential indeed."

"What does influential mean?" asks Kais.
"It means someone who has a huge impact in making something happen." Mr. Leon smiles.
"Oh," replies Kais. "I get it."
"Now, the man I want to tell you about was even more influential, but much less known. You could say that Dr. King and Malcolm X stood on his shoulders."

"Really? Like Frederick Douglass?"
"Close! His name was Toussaint Louverture," Mr. Leon says.
"Two what?" Kais scrunches his brows.

"Toussaint Louverture. His father was brought from Africa as a slave to a small island called Saint-Domingue (now Haiti), where Toussaint was born in 1743. Nonetheless, unlike you, Toussaint didn't receive a proper education."

Kais couldn't believe his ears. "But every child should receive an education?"

Mr. Leon nods. "Indeed, Kais, but slave owners feared the idea of an educated slave. They were afraid that basic reading and writing skills could empower the slaves to organize and revolt."
Kais felt bad for the slaves. "Then how did he become so influential if he had no education?" Kais asks.

"As Toussaint grew older, he became very curious. His godfather secretly taught him to read. He also learned to ride horses and became the caretaker of the livestock in the whole Breda Plantation. Eventually, he hired a French tutor and read every book he could get his hands on, especially those by French philosophers who spoke against inequality. He surprised his masters and other whites with his knowledge and charisma, and in 1776, he became a free man."

"Were all the slaves freed?" Kais asks, hope gleaming in his eyes.
Mr. Leon shakes his head. "No, just a very small number of skilled ones. They had to fight for their freedom and a lot of them died."

Discretely reading the master's newspapers, Toussaint discovered the news about the French Revolution, which succeeded under the principle that every man is now equal.

Toussaint convinced those in Saint-Domingue that this principle was worth fighting for. He'd talk about the Bible which he read often. The Bible never said that God created the white man in His image but every man, he added. With words like these, he mustered an army.

Kais saw that Toussaint was no ordinary man.

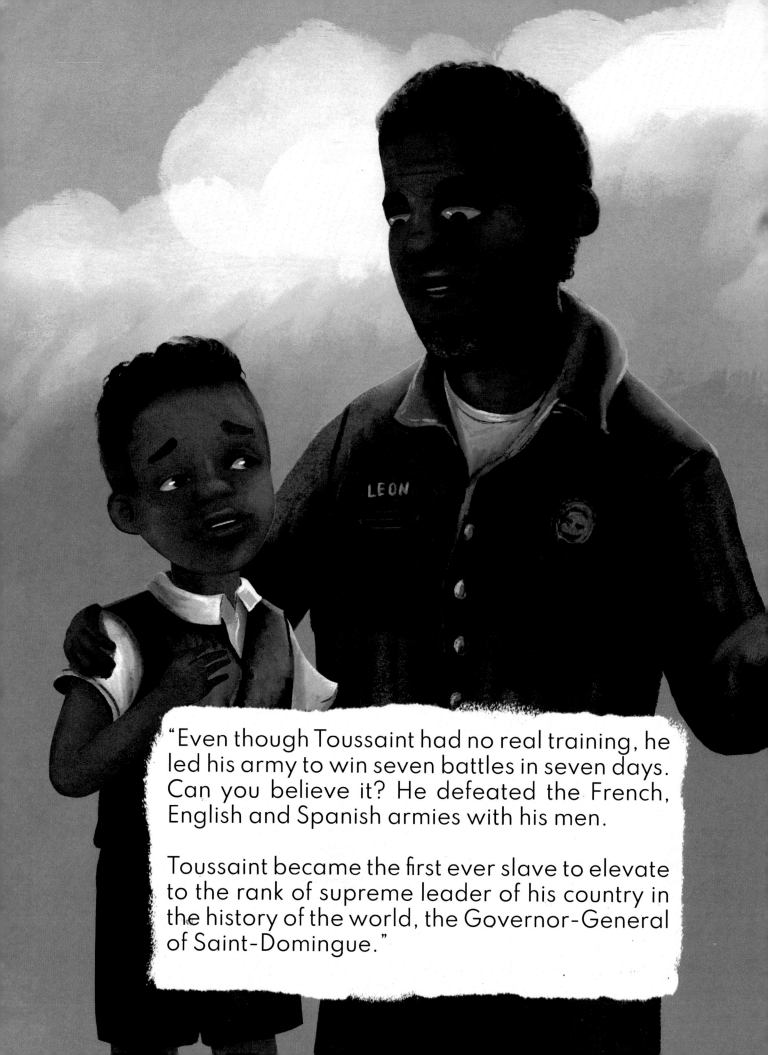

"Even though Toussaint had no real training, he led his army to win seven battles in seven days. Can you believe it? He defeated the French, English and Spanish armies with his men.

Toussaint became the first ever slave to elevate to the rank of supreme leader of his country in the history of the world, the Governor-General of Saint-Domingue."

Kais was amazed. "And the slaves were free?"
"Yes, and instead of seeking revenge on the masters, Toussaint sought to fix a broken system. During slavery, Saint-Domingue was by far the most prosperous colony. Between 1793-1801, Toussaint encouraged the former slaves to work for profit. He told them that a free man is one

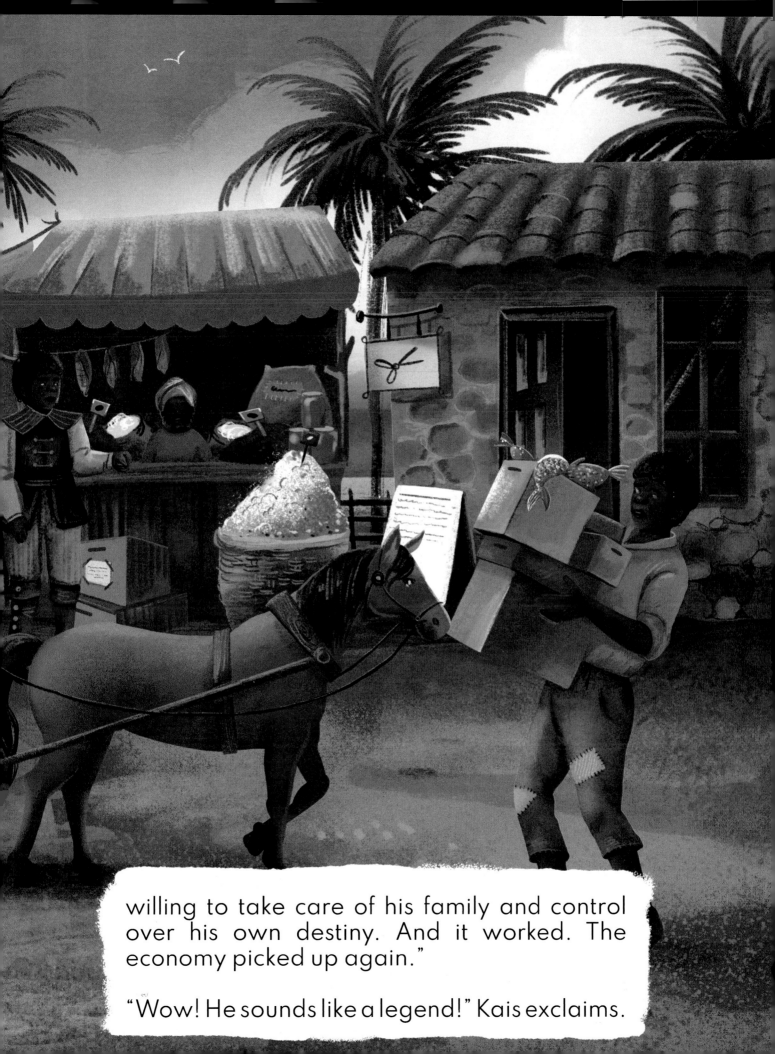

willing to take care of his family and control over his own destiny. And it worked. The economy picked up again."

"Wow! He sounds like a legend!" Kais exclaims.

Mr. Leon smiles. "Yes, Toussaint left behind quite the legacy. In an attempt to reinstate slavery, the French captured him in 1802 and he was transported to an underground freezing jail in France, called Fort de Joux. However, before boarding the ship, he said, 'In chasing me from my land, you have only cut the tree's trunk. It will continue to grow by its roots for they are deep and numerous.'

"President who?" Kais asked.
"Precedent. The first. The one to show the way. Aboli-tionists in the US drew inspiration from this revolution and were directly supported by the Haitians."

Addressing a crowd at the dedication of the Haitian pavilion at the World's Columbian Exposition in Chicago in 1893, Frederick Douglass said, and I quote:

"We should not forget that the freedom you and I enjoy today is largely due to the brave stand taken by the black sons of Haiti ninety years ago. Striking for their freedom, they struck for the freedom of every black man in the world."

Kais nodded. "What a fascinating story! Thank you for teaching me all this Mr. Leon."
"It was my pleasure young man."
"But how do you know so much about Toussaint?" asks Kais.

Mr. Leon looked away. "I used to be a history professor in Haiti. When I moved to this country, schools wouldn't hire me because of my foreign training. And so, I am here, still contributing to a place of learning."

"Oh, okay," Kais slowly replied. "Well, that doesn't seem right. You've taught me a lot, Mr. Leon. Thank you."

"Of course, Kais." Carrying his mop, Mr. Leon starts to round the corner. "See you around kiddo."

"Bye," says Kais, and he turns toward the front office.

The secretary waves as he enters. "Hey there, Kais! Your mom is just finishing up." "Thank you!" he replies. "Hey, Mom. I was wondering if you found a new librarian yet. I have an idea."

Notes to Parents and Educators

Kristin developed the storyline for this book the day Kais, as a grade two assignment for black history month, wrote about George Washington as a noteworthy figure for black people. There are so many exceptional characters and role models our children should know, from every corner of the earth. We encourage you to dig and find the heroes of your heritage and make their story known.

In 2017 when I visited the National Museum of African American History and Culture, I was proud and encouraged by the exhibits about Toussaint Louverture and the Haitian revolution. This acknowledgment gave me hope that American citizens would learn this aspect of Haitian history and how it contributed to the emancipation efforts in the US. Toussaint was chasing the indisputable truth that everyone is equal and that no man should ever have been the property of another.

Haiti and France

Haiti achieved its freedom from France in 1804 after 13 years of insurrection. It was the first country to liberate itself from slavery. Two decades later in 1825, France threatened the newly liberated nation with military invasion if the Haitian government refused to pay an indemnity adjusted approximately to 28 billion dollars of today's currency to compensate them for the property value they had lost during the Haitian revolution which included Haitian slaves and plantations. These devastating reparations led to a budget that could never balance as Haiti struggled for 122 years to repay the debt, with interest financed through French banks and US based Citybank. Paying approximately 80% of its GDP annually towards this debt left very little resources for developing infrastructure. Imagine trying to establish roadways, healthcare and education systems or a thriving domestic economy with only 20 cents of every dollar. Haiti had been regarded as the pearl of the Caribbean, the most resource filled of all the Antilles but this potential was never achieved, becoming increasingly dependent on imports and aid rather than developing a strong self-sufficient economy.

Haiti and the USA

President John Adams saw in Governor Toussaint Louverture a partner in trade and strategic diplomacy in the region between 1798-1801. He treated him with equal respect as his white counterparts, however his successor Thomas Jefferson in 1801 had a different perception of Toussaint and the free blacks of Haiti. For the 6 decades thereafter, the US refused to trade with Haiti. Knowing the measure would have crippled Haiti's economy, the US government also chose to side with the French as those free blacks of Haiti were perceived as a threat to the million still enslaved in the South at the time. Now, less than 700 miles from the southern shores of Florida, somewhere in the Caribbean, they would become free citizens as the Haitian founding fathers have pronounced in their constitution, offering their country as a haven, a welcoming destination for the oppressed. This explains why Frederick Douglass had contemplated relocating to Haiti along with daughter Rosetta when he finally lost all hope in the emancipation process, right before the civil war. Haiti also overturned the notion that blacks were inferior to whites as black Haitians defeated arguably the strongest white army of the time.

Current Conditions

Unfortunately in Haiti there is not a functional democracy; the electoral process is malignantly corrupt. The electoral council itself was unconstitutionally assembled before the 2010 elections. Most importantly, its president was charged with bribery and corruption during the process and reported coercion from certain western countries and international organizations to select a losing candidate to the run-off who eventually became president. For example, France would not support a candidate who planned to seek restitution of the 28 billion ransom they robbed Haitians of for reclaiming their liberty. The vote of the people for the most capable and honest leaders never mattered.

Elected officials and dictatorships have further derailed progress by mishandling the country's economy favoring friends, families and interest groups to the detriment of all the people, leaving most of the country living in poverty.

An estimated 6 million Haitians live below the poverty level with $2.41/day and more than 2.5 million people below the severe poverty level of $1.12/day. Those numbers in 2021 have deteriorated significantly due to the staggering increase in inflation, chronic corruption and depreciation of the local currency. This is directly related to a staggering unemployment rate of 42% and a national literacy rate around only 60% with a very poor quality of education in some instances. As of 2021, the average Haitian teacher makes 3.4 to 4 dollars a day. More than 80% of the very small proportion that completed a higher education is forced to leave the country in search of stable employment. Many young men and women felt compelled to risk their lives to travel illegally to the Dominican Republic, Chile, Brazil, some in the hope to make it to the US just to look for a job they could have easily done in their own country. While Haiti shares the same island (Hispanola) as the Dominican Republic and offers equally gorgeous mountains and beaches, it garners less than 20% of the tourism dollars as the Dominican Republic. Critical thinking Haitians ask themselves how any country can develop if no effort is made to educate and invest in its children until they realize that the plan has never been for the country to develop but to serve the rich and powerful. Yet all these children belong to the lineage of Toussaint and Dessalines and should be thriving in the fruits of their struggles.

Nevertheless, there is still hope. A group of integrity-prone, anticorruption young leaders, a lot of them female, risk their lives on a daily basis in order to fight for the voiceless. During 2020-2021 so many freedom fighters have fallen including Gregory St Hilaire who was assassinated inside of his university and Antoinette Duclaire, a social activist who was very vocal against corruption within the establishment. We will continue to join our voices to theirs until Haiti becomes a place where everyone can prosper, not just the few rich and powerful. Education and the fight against corruption are our way out of poverty.

Words In Action

To help bridge the gap between potential and the stagnant lack of resources and infrastructure, even for one village, I started Words In Action in 2008. The foundation (a registered 501c3) operates a medical clinic in the mountain hamlet of QuiCroit. It also provides scholarship for over 100 students including 12 university students with the plan to return to their community after graduation. Further projects include rebuilding the local school, improving teacher training and developing a library. All the proceeds of this book support these projects, to build lasting pathways to development. To learn more, we welcome you to visit wiahaiti.org.

About the Authors

Claude is a family medicine physician, the 2021 Medical Society of Virginia Salute to Service Award winner recognized for "Service to the International Community". He is the founder of "Words In Action" which operates a community clinic and a school sponsorship program in Qui-Croit, Haiti. His first children book "I'm All Grown Now, Papa" is a children's memoir of his childhood in the mountains of Haiti. Kristin, his wife is a loving mother, a dietitian and his co-author on this project. She has always supported his dedication to help the children of his community receive an education and achieve their potential. Kristin proposed writing children's books to help finance the sponsorship program. They both enjoy being active, spending time outside and reading with their children.

About the Illustrator

Anastasiia Yezhela is a professional illustrator of children's books from Kyiv, Ukraine. She creates vibrant books that touch the hearts of thousands of children and parents around the world. Anastastiia is inspired by travel. The best ideas come to her when she travels. She believes that love is the most powerful in this world: "All the best was done out of love for God, people or loved ones."

Made in the USA
Monee, IL
02 June 2022

97361053R00024